The Process: Your Path to Financial Wellness

Jim Hanna

Copyright © 2016 Jim Hanna

All rights reserved.

ISBN-13: 978-0-9978023-1-3

Retire With Jim Hanna Wealth Advisors

Phone: 210-641-5000
Fax: 210-547-7980
Email: info@RetireWithJimHanna.com
Website www.RetireWithJimHanna.com

JIM HANNA

Retire with Jim Hanna *is an independent financial services firm helping individuals create retirement strategies using a variety of investment and insurance products to suit their needs.*

Investment advisory services are offered through AE Wealth Management, LLC, an SEC Registered Investment Adviser.

This publication contains the opinions and ideas of its author. The strategies outlined in this book may not be suitable for every individual and are not guaranteed or warranted to produce any particular results. The author is not an attorney, and does not give legal advice.

This book is sold with the understanding that neither publisher, nor author through this book, is engaged in rendering legal advice, tax advice, investment, insurance, financial, accounting, or any other professional advice or services. If the reader requires such advice or services, a competent professional should be consulted. Relevant laws vary from state to state.

No warranty is made with respect to the accuracy or the completeness of the information contained herein, and both the author and the publisher specifically disclaim any responsibility for any liability, loss, or risk, personal or otherwise, that is incurred as a consequence, directly or indirectly, of the use and application of any of the contents of this book.

This book is written under the right of the First Amendment to the Constitution of the United States. This book is written as an outside business activity from my investment, advisory, and securities business. The ideas expressed are not meant to be taken as advice that you can act on. You should find an individual advisor that you trust to implement these ideas after determining if they are appropriate and suitable for your unique situation.

Insurance products and annuities are guaranteed by the insurance companies themselves. The safety of these accounts is dependent on the claims' paying ability of the insurance companies.

Investing involves risk, including the potential loss of principal. No investment strategy can guarantee a profit or protect against loss in periods of declining values. None of the information contained in this book will constitute an offer to sell or solicit any offer to buy a security or any insurance product.

Any references to steady and reliable or lifetime income streams in this book refer only to fixed insurance products. They do not refer, in any way, to securities or investment advisory products, and are not offered by AE Wealth Management, LLC. Annuity guarantees are backed by the financial strength and claims-paying ability of the issuing insurance company. Annuities are insurance products that may be subject to fees, surrender charges and holding periods which vary by insurance company. Annuities are not FDIC insured.

The information and opinions contained herein provided by third parties have been obtained from sources believed to be reliable, but accuracy and completeness cannot be guaranteed.

The author as well as the information provided in this book are not related to, endorsed by, nor connected with and not approved by any government agency or organization. For information regarding your Social Security benefits, you are encouraged to speak to your local Social Security Administration office or visit the Social Security Administration website at www.ssa.gov.

JIM HANNA

ACKNOWLEDGMENTS

First I would like to thank my wife, Barbie, for her support, love and patience throughout all the years of my busy six day work week schedule.

Next, a thank you to all of our clients for their confidence in our firm, for the continued business and the referral of friends and family.

Finally, a thank you to my assistant, Irma Lewis. Her contributions for the past eight years have been essential to the success of this company.

JIM HANNA

CONTENTS

	Preface	i
	Introduction	1
Chapter 1	Typical client profile	9
Chapter 2	Typical concerns of our clients	19
Chapter 3	What you need to know before your first appointment	33
Chapter 4	Our first meeting: getting to know you	41
Chapter 5	Our second meeting: working on a solution	51
Chapter 6	Our third meeting: finalizing the details	67
Chapter 7	Choosing the right financial advisor for you	73
Chapter 8	Red flags in a financial advisor	85
Chapter 9	Jim Hanna's team: ambassador experience	93

PREFACE

"I've always been taught to think that vulnerability meant weakness. What I've learned today is that vulnerability is relatability...and relatability is where connections are forged. We've been taught all wrong in this industry. We prop ourselves up with "credentials" and "accolades" and "expertise." People don't connect to me because of the letters after my name.

When it comes to people, TRUST is more powerful than knowledge. People don't initially TRUST me because I know things. They TRUST me because they can RELATE to me."

- Matthew Neuman

INTRODUCTION

This was a difficult book to write. Financial planning and retirement concepts are highly technical by definition. If you have ever glanced at a book about investing, you have probably seen complex phrases like "equity investments that give up some upside to get more protection on the downside" and "include derivatives to future-proof your portfolio". If you did not understand those, that is OK. They are enough to make my head spin, and I work with investments for a living.

As the idea for this book took shape, I realized that I have two problems with financial planning books. First of all, most of them are just too complex. I like short sentences, clear examples, and plain English. I have discovered that there are few books on the shelves that match my preference.

Second, most financial planning books are written as reference manuals. They are crammed with technical terms, scenarios, and present value calculations. Some of the material may be relevant to you today, but let's be honest – virtually no one reads those books cover to cover. You might flip to a chapter that matters (Social Security strategies, for example), skim it, and hope to take away enough meaningful tips to make it worth your time.

This book is different.

To start, I wanted it to be an easy read for you - 2 to 4 hours at the most. I have also stayed away from words like "alpha" or "optimizing present value of future cash flows". You will find that I have chosen simple words and used lots of client stories to illustrate my points. These stories do not represent an endorsement by such clients of my firm or the products and services we provide. I have, of course, altered the names of the clients to protect their identities. You will find the text of this book easy to follow and simple to remember.

An easy read does not necessarily make this an easy subject. When you consider your financial strategy, you are thinking about money and death – two topics that aren't usually discussed. Most people are not taught how to talk about money and death, so their instinct is to simply stay out of the conversation.

That approach has landed us in some hot water as a nation. Many Americans today are woefully unprepared for retirement. Here are a few statistics for you.

- 28% of Americans have saved less than $1,000 for their retirement.[1]

- 54% of Americans have too little saved to establish an income stream in retirement, which means they can never stop working.[2]

- In 1983, over 60% of working Americans had some kind of a pension plan from their employer. Today, fewer than 20% have access to a plan, and most have to rely on Social Security as a primary

---

[1] Employee Benefit Research Institute (EBRI) 2015 study,
http://www.fool.com/investing/general/2015/12/06/the-average-american-is-woefully-unprepared-for-re.aspx

[2] Schwartz Center for Economic Policy Analysis at the New School
http://www.forbes.com/sites/laurashin/2015/04/09/the-retirement-crisis-why-68-of-americans-arent-saving-in-an-employer-sponsored-plan/#527bb1a519d8

source of income in retirement.[3]

Combine those statistics with a longer life expectancy as more Americans are living into their 90's, and running out of money in retirement becomes a real issue.

The situation is caused in large part by companies moving away from pension plans towards 401K plans. In effect, that has shifted the planning responsibility to people who are not trained or qualified to make investment decisions. However, some of the blame also rests with our widespread unwillingness to face the money questions.

Here is what I want for you to take away after finishing this book.

---

[3] http://www.mybudget360.com/millions-of-americans-unprepared-for-retirement-savings-retirement-pensions-americans/

- I want you to have a basic understanding of concepts that are important for your financial independence in retirement. With those ideas absorbed and integrated, you will be able to have an intelligent conversation about your financial future.
- I want you to understand how to choose a financial advisor. You may choose to work with me, stay with your current advisor, or go somewhere else. The important thing is that you will have the information and the tools to make an intelligent choice when it comes to selecting the professional who will support you and your family through good times and bad.
- I want you to know when to walk away from an advisor. According to a Boston-based research group Cerulli Associates, there are just under

300,000 financial advisors across the United States.[4] As in any profession, there are amazing advisors, average ones, and bad ones. I want you to be educated and empowered so that you are never taken advantage of. You have worked too hard for this money to lose it because of bad advice.

Why do you need financial advice?

Here is how I see it. If you have a back pain or a debilitating headache, at some point you will probably find your way to a doctor's office. You might sit in the reception area and fill out some paperwork to describe your symptoms. Then, you will meet your doctor. He will examine you, ask you questions, and run some tests in an effort to figure

---

[4] http://www.reuters.com/article/wealth-cerulli-advisor-headcount-idUSL1N0VL23920150211

out what is wrong. Then, he will issue a diagnosis and recommend a treatment plan to help you feel better.

As a financial advisor, I do the same thing for your finances. We talk about where you are right now, and what concerns you might have. Most people come to me because they are unsure they can retire, scared of the rising costs of medical care, and terrified of what would happen to their spouse when they pass on. Your concerns might fall along the same lines, or they might be different. No matter what, I listen, ask questions, and offer my recommendations. If we decide to work together, I hold your hand and support you as we implement your financial strategy.

CHAPTER 1

TYPICAL CLIENT PROFILE

I will open this chapter by saying that we work with all kinds of clients. Married couples, single people, divorced people, widows and widowers, career military folks – we have seen and been fortunate enough to help them with some, if not all, aspects of their finances. Many of them are in their 50's or older, most have 401K and IRA savings, and some have inherited money.

Regardless of their personal circumstances, here are some scenarios that typically bring new clients to our office.

- Death of a parent
- Marriage or divorce

- Buying or selling a house
- Legacy planning
- Complex financial products, such as long term care insurance
- Upcoming retirement

If some of those scenarios look familiar, you should know that your financial and emotional outcomes could be improved by engaging the assistance of an independent financial professional. Studies have shown that an average investor produces worse results than a market index because average investors are prone to panic and make bad decisions when the market hits a bump.[5] In my experience, the vast majority of people are not trained to be effective at

---

[5] DALBAR QAIB 2015

making complex financial decisions. Investing is not all that different from re-wiring your house or doing dental work – beyond the basics, most of us are wise to seek advice from trained professionals.

What can hold you back from coming in to see a financial advisor? Here is a story from one of our clients, Theresa, who came to us after a divorce, at age 60.

Theresa came to us very distressed. She and her husband had just divorced after 28 years of marriage. Theresa had stayed home to take care of the couple's children, so her own working history was limited to a few part-time jobs outside of the home. Theresa's husband had always managed their joint financial affairs, and she hadn't been involved in any money decisions.

As a result of her divorce settlement, Theresa received a lump sum of money from her ex-husband. She had no idea what to do next. After figuring out her monthly expenses, Theresa understood that the settlement money would only last about 7 years if she simply deposited it into her checking account and used it to cover her bills. Theresa had no pension, and as far as she knew her monthly Social Security payment would amount to only $600 at age 66 – not nearly enough to afford housing and medical care, let alone food and utilities.

Theresa felt embarrassed to come in and visit with us sooner because she didn't want to look foolish. What ultimately brought her in is the clarity that without a professional review and a plan, she would simply run out of money. At 60 years old, Theresa wasn't ready to go back to school to learn a new trade in the hopes of securing better than minimum pay. Theresa was hopeful that something could be done to improve her situation.

We met with Theresa to talk through her circumstances and look at her accounts. We showed her some ways of creating a steady and reliable cash flow while still keeping plenty of emergency money on hand.

We also explained her options for getting a larger Social Security check. Theresa didn't know she could receive half of her ex-husband's Social Security benefit payment, which would equal $1,200 per month – much better than $600!

Our timely involvement allowed the client to maintain the lifestyle she was accustomed to, and to retire knowing that there would be enough money to cover her living expenses and more. In matters of money, time is your ally – and more of it is better. With more time, we have the luxury of a deeper tool box of options. So, it is always best to have a conversation sooner rather than later.

Here is another client story, this time from a couple.

Daniel and Sandra came to us with retirement looming on the horizon, and no plan to speak of.

After a 31 year career, Daniel was facing retirement. He had been diligently contributing to his 401K for most of his career, and had accumulated about $400,000. It was time to make decisions about what to do with that money, and he wanted to explore his options.

Daniel was especially concerned about his pension payment option, because it only paid a fixed monthly amount with no access to the $400K account value. It also had limited survivor benefits. If Daniel passed away before Sandra, she would only receive half of his pension with no access to the account value. If they both passed away, their children would receive nothing, and the account balance would be absorbed by the plan sponsor. As Daniel put it, "If we both die in a few years, most of my hard earned money will be for nothing."

We showed Daniel and Sandra a variety of tools

available to address these issues. We considered lifetime income, survivor benefits, liquidity concerns, and the legacy the couple wanted to leave for their children. Following our advice, Daniel was able to take the lump sum amount from his 401K, and use most of that to create a steady and reliable income stream using the tools we provided. He retained enough easy-access money in the event of a financial emergency, and gained a better spousal benefit. The couple would also be able to pass the unused funds to their heirs.

When you have your back against the wall, or have just been through a stressful experience of a loved one passing, a divorce, or a medical diagnosis, it is easy to feel as if you have no good choices left. As independent financial professionals, our job is to

THE PROCESS: YOUR PATH TO FINANCIAL WELLNESS

find and show you every option you have, and give you the information and the confidence to choose the right one.

CHAPTER 2

TYPICAL CONCERNS OF OUR CLIENTS

Just as you go to a doctor when something hurts or does not work, so do many of our clients. As we have talked with thousands of people over the years, we have noticed that their concerns can be mapped into five categories. Everyone's situation is a little different, and every person's mix of concerns is unique. However, here are some common patterns. As you are preparing for your visit with a financial advisor, you may find this list helpful to organize your thoughts.

Will I be able to afford my healthcare?

This question is not surprising. As we get older, we

tend to need more doctors' visits, tests, medications, hospital stays, and physical therapy sessions. Just needing more medical services and products wouldn't be so bad if they were not getting more expensive every year. Studies have shown that increases in medical costs have outpaced general inflation every year since 2009.[6]

The good news is that retirees have options when it comes to their healthcare. From Medicare to Medigap insurance, making the right choices can help you buy the optimal amount of coverage at a fair premium amount. However, you must consider application timing – applying for certain policies late can result in penalties, and may even cost you the

---

[6] http://www.forbes.com/sites/mikepatton/2015/06/29/u-s-health-care-costs-rise-faster-than-inflation/#4a4a90776ad2

opportunity to get coverage. You must also think through your immediate and future needs. Healthcare coverage is a complex topic, and if you have any concerns about your ability to afford coverage, or are unsure whether you have enough coverage, you need to talk to a professional.

A decision to buy long-term care insurance fits into this category, as well. Here is a client story to illustrate the importance of thinking through your options carefully.

Anna is 85. She was living on her own in San Antonio, enjoying an active and independent lifestyle and only a few health problems. Last summer she stepped on a pebble while walking outside. Her foot rolled out from under her, and Anna fell. A broken hip and several fractures later, and Anna's prognosis was clear: she could no longer live on her own. Anna's physician recommended a move to an assisted living community. Anna thought that was a good next step, and was looking forward to meeting new people and having help. There was only one problem - Anna didn't have a long term care policy.

So far, Anna had been able to pay for her expenses by using Social Security benefits and her limited savings. She didn't qualify for Medicaid. The assisted living facility would cost $50,000 a year, of which Anna could cover $10,000. Anna was out of ideas.

As Anna's situation demonstrates, the cost of long term care can be high. The problem is that premiums for long-term care insurance don't look much better. Many policies come with restrictions and limitations, as well as a "use it or lose it" clause. In other words, if you don't end up needing long term care, you will have paid your hard-earned money for a peace of mind and not much more. A professional can guide you through your options, including hybrid policies that include a life insurance-like component, as well as buying shared long-term care insurance for a couple.

Will I outlive my money?

With Americans living longer, and lacking the traditional pension plans that used to supplement their Social Security payments in retirement, running out of money is a real concern. Answering the question of whether one is able to retire is really about comparing the assets (anticipated Social Security payments, 401K balances, and any other possible sources of income) with lifestyle expenses, and structuring a way to match the two. This is where a consultation with a financial advisor can be invaluable.

John and Sarah are 62 years old. Retirement is getting closer, so they have decided to get organized and take a look at what their income stream and expenses might look like once they stop working.

Their current lifestyle, between housing, transportation, medical care, and other expenses, costs about $6,000 per month. The couple can expect about $4,200 per month in Social Security benefits. John and Sarah are currently renting a small carriage house in their back yard to a tenant, which brings in another $350 per month. Between their Social Security and the monthly rent income, they will be short $1,450 per month. If they were to lose the tenant, the gap would grow to $1,800 per month.

John and Sarah have an additional potential source of income. They have been contributing for years to an IRA, and the account stands at $350,000. It is invested in a mix of stocks and mutual funds. That might seem like a lot of money, but simply using the IRA balance to cover the conservative gap of $1,800 monthly means that the balance will run out in a little over 16 years. Assuming no growth in the IRA, that is the best case scenario! After considering taxes and the possibility of negative market fluctuations, the IRA balance does not look nearly as healthy. John and Sarah could withdraw the money from the IRA today and put it in a savings account, but that would have triggered a tax event and put them in a higher tax bracket.

Now what?

The answer will be unique and specific to each situation. In some cases, we are able to create a steady and reliable source of income that covers the shortfall between the Social Security benefit and the lifestyle expenses. Strategic choices about when to claim Social Security can make a difference. No one likes to talk about cutting expenses, but sometimes it takes an independent advisor to look at your monthly outflows and help you get smart about money so that you have enough for what matters to you.

Will my savings go straight to the tax man?

Some people mistakenly believe that their tax expenses will decrease in retirement. With advance tax and cash flow planning, that can be the case – however, it is not something that happens automatically. That was true for John and Sarah – had they simply withdrawn the shortfall money out of their IRA, the tax consequences would have wiped out a good portion of their savings. At our practice, we consider the tax impact of every recommendation and decision we make, and work with qualified tax advisors so that our clients are never surprised by a tax bill.

Should I be invested in the stock market right now?

Watching the ups and downs of the market is not for the faint of heart. A lot of pre-retirees have a portion of their portfolio in specific stocks or index funds, so those dips and slides represent real money to them.

I like this quote by A. Gary Shilling: *"Markets can remain irrational a lot longer than you and I can remain solvent."* If you are nearing your retirement, you must pay attention to how much of your money is subject to the market risk. The stock market growth game is all about time, and no one wants to pull money out at the bottom of the market. Here is a story to illustrate it.

Linda is a single mother who is 55 years old. She has a 20 year old daughter Jenny, who has just landed her first corporate job. Jenny's employer offers a 401K plan, and matches contributions after the first year of full-time work. Jenny is smart to take advantage of this opportunity. She begins to contribute to her 401K plan right away - after all, the employer's contribution is basically free money!

Jenny's 401K contributions are invested in a mix of stocks and mutual funds. Over the years, the balance certainly has the potential to grow at a faster rate than it would if she were to simply put that money in a savings account. The market roller-coaster will make the balance drop and rise over the years, but that does not matter to Jenny. She can afford to take a risk, because she is 40+ years away from needing to use that money.

Linda's situation is different. With fewer than 10 years before retirement, she needs to watch her risks more carefully. As she gets older, she would be wise to shift a larger portion of her investments to a lower-risk bucket where a market hiccup won't derail her plans.

What will happen to my spouse when I die?

We hear this question a lot, and for good reason. Very often, families delegate money decisions to one spouse. He or she meets with the investment advisor, chooses the mutual funds to invest in, and keeps track of the various accounts across brokerage firms and banks. The other spouse typically trusts his or her judgment and does not get involved.

This arrangement is convenient, right up to the point where the decision maker passes. Let's imagine that the husband managed all money decisions for the family. Upon his passing, the widow is typically left with no idea of where to begin. Was there a will? Where should she look for various accounts? Was her name on any of those accounts, and can she access them? What should she do with the balances?

The way we approach this situation is by working with the couple together, from the very first days. If we assume that the husband is the primary decision maker on financial matters, we bring the wife into the conversation, make sure all of her questions are answered, and build a relationship with her – because this money will likely be hers one day, and we want for her to be informed and in control.

CHAPTER 3

WHAT YOU NEED TO KNOW BEFORE YOUR FIRST APPOINTMENT

A lot of our new clients come in for their first appointment with a mix of nervousness and apprehension. Having helped hundreds of clients over the years, we understand how you feel, and do everything we can to create a friendly and relaxing environment for you.

I want you to have a great first experience with us. Being prepared and knowing what to expect is a big part of it. So, think of this appointment as a visit to a "financial doctor". Maybe you already work with an advisor and want a second opinion, or perhaps you have never worked with a financial professional before. Regardless of what happened in the past, I want you to know that you have made a good decision. The hour you have taken out of your busy day to spend in our office will be a good investment of your time.

Here is a client story that illustrates it.

A client of ours, named Joe, is married to his sweetheart Melanie. Two years ago, Melanie was diagnosed with leukemia. The couple joined forces as Melanie went through the first rounds of chemotherapy, only to discover that the drugs mysteriously stopped working 6 months into it.

Joe insisted on getting a second opinion, and found a different oncologist who diagnosed the problem (an obscure problem with liver enzymes) and proposed a solution. The new treatment plan stabilized Melanie's condition. If it were not for Joe's quick thinking and insistence on getting another professional involved, Melanie would not be alive today.

Second opinions matter, whether it comes to your medical condition or financial health. If your current financial strategy is robust and your advisor is doing a great job, we will tell you that – in fact, it does happen with quite a few of our first-time visitors.

I encourage you to use this opportunity to the maximum. Getting a slot on a financial advisor's calendar can be just as difficult as finding an opening to see a medical specialist – don't waste this valuable chance to potentially improve your situation.

People often ask me what they need to know before our first meeting. A few simple things come to mind.

Remember that the goal of this meeting is simply to get to know each other.

Financial advisors can have a bad reputation of being like used car salesmen, pushing complex products and investment options just to earn commissions. This is not how we work.

A word you need to know in regards to how we operate is "fiduciary". I know I had promised no technical words, but this one is really important. What it means is that we have a legal and moral obligation to put your interests above everything else. Our goal is getting the best outcome for you and your family. Period.

We have a duty of care to you as our client. That means no confusing information or terminology. We use our experience and the best practices of the entire industry to offer prudent and accurate advice.

We also have a duty of loyalty, which means that all of our actions and recommendations are in your best interest. Not because this product pays a bigger commission, and not because we have a relationship with this dealer, but because this is the best choice for you. These are not just words – it is a legal responsibility that we accept with honor, because we believe this is the only right way to serve our clients.

Whenever possible, we involve you and your spouse in conversation together.

As I have mentioned earlier, most families designate

one person to be in charge of financial decisions. That is fine and good, but at the end of the day it is often the other spouse who has to put the pieces together after the original decision-maker has passed on.

We want both of you to know and understand what is going on. That is not just lip service, either – we spend a good portion of the meeting getting to know each one of you, so that we can support you both in whatever comes next.

Our approach is holistic.

That means we look at and can work with other professionals, including tax advisors and attorneys, in your or our network to advise you on all aspects of your finances: legal, tax, financial planning, business succession, family relationships, and health care. You are one person, and it would not be fair or wise to propose a financial strategy based on just one piece of your situation.

Our approach is slow and patient.

One thing you don't have to worry about is us trying to sell you an obscure investment out of the gate. There are no high-pressure tactics, and no one will rush you into decisions that you are not ready for.

We only want to work with clients in situations where we can help them pursue their financial goals, and where our approach is a good fit for their personality. If we are going to work together, it will be a true partnership and collaboration, and we come into the first appointment with that premise.

JIM HANNA

CHAPTER 4

OUR FIRST MEETING:

GETTING TO KNOW YOU

The first thing you need to know about our introductory meeting (sometimes we refer to it as our "discovery meeting") is that you have chosen to be there.

Yes, that's right. Just as in a situation with getting a second opinion from a medical doctor, you understood the value of dedicating an hour out of your busy day to sit down and talk about your financial situation.

Some clients come to us because they have an obvious or urgent dilemma they need help with – perhaps their parents have passed on and left them money, or maybe a divorce has left them without the usual safety net. Those clients can be compared to people in the hospital emergency room that have a broken leg or severe chest pains. As much as they would like to, they physically cannot be anywhere else until their urgent situation is stabilized.

Others come in without urgent symptoms – either because something vaguely does not seem right, or because they need reassurance that they are on the right path. They can stand to benefit just as much as the "emergency room" clients do. In some cases their potential benefit is actually greater. Because we do not have to rush to stop the client's "pain" in an emergency situation, we have the luxury of working towards optimization of an already decent situation.

No matter which camp you land in, I urge you to remember that your time and mine is valuable. You would not simply skip a medical specialist appointment that you had waited 2 months to get! Your money is no less important. You are here to get the confidence and the comfort that comes from knowing (not just hoping) that your family is as well protected as you think it is. That is worth a lot. That is why I come to work every morning. I need you to show up so that I can help you.

What should you expect from our first meeting?

The best way to answer that is to explain the typical flow of the meeting. I will ask you questions, listen to your story, and ask more questions. This is not my time to do nuts and bolts planning. It is my opportunity to get to know you and your family.

Remember the word "fiduciary" that I had mentioned in the previous chapter? That is the reason the first meeting is all about you. I am legally and morally obligated to give you the best possible advice for your situation. In order to do that, I must know everything there is to know about your circumstances.

Some of the questions may seem easy or obvious – don't let that confuse you, just answer them anyway. I don't want to have to guess or fill in the blanks on my own, and my review or strategy is always more accurate if you give me the puzzle pieces.

Some questions may seem difficult, deeply personal, and scary. Again, I simply need you to do your best in answering them. I am not asking these questions to put you in a tight spot and watch you squirm – this is about my ability to give you the best advice my experience and expertise can offer. If you are genuinely uncomfortable answering a question, don't be afraid to say so. You are in control of the conversation.

Every single discovery meeting is different, and none of them are scripted. They could not possibly be – or how would I ever hope to get to know the exceptionally diverse clients that I am blessed to help? However, the conversation does have a typical flow to it. Here are some of the questions that I may ask. Please use these as a rough guide to thinking through your personal and financial circumstances.

Questions about your family situation:

- Are you married? Divorced? Is this your second or third marriage?
- Do you have any children? How old are they? Are any of them special needs?
- Do you need to set aside any money for education expenses?
- Where do your parents live? How old are they, and how is their health?
- Do you have any siblings? What is your relationship like?

Question about your retirement:

- When are you hoping to retire?
- What about retirement is most important to you?
- What do you picture yourself doing after you

stop working?

- What is your biggest concern or fear when you think about retirement?
- How do you feel about your money situation?

Personal questions:

- What is your health like? Are there any medical issues that I should know about to give you the best advice?
- What is your social life like?
- What do you enjoy doing?
- Do you have any loans or debt?
- Do you have an emergency "rainy day" fund?
- What is your plan in the event of a serious or prolonged illness?

- Have you had any bad experiences with investing?
- What about money is most important to you?

If you are a veteran, I will ask you questions about your length of service and other details. I have personally helped veterans and spouses who had been told they did not qualify for military benefits when in fact they did. It is my responsibility to ensure that you have considered every possible income source.

Some clients like to bring documents along to our first meeting. I find that having statements ready can help us look up a number or clarify a question ("Whose name is on that bank account?")

THE PROCESS: YOUR PATH TO FINANCIAL WELLNESS

Here is a list of paperwork that you may consider bringing to the first appointment.

- Most recent statements for your accounts (bank accounts, 401K accounts, IRAs, 529's);
- Compensation details (pay stubs, Social Security statements, pension paperwork, inheritance amount);
- Monthly expenses, including household bills and credit cards;
- Most recent tax records, and
- Estate planning documents (will, trust).

The first meeting will conclude with us choosing a convenient time for the second appointment.

That's right, you do not typically walk away with a

prescription after the first examination! There are some rare situations where the issue is straightforward and the solution is simple, in which case I may be able to offer my recommendations on the spot. In most cases, I need time to mull over everything I have learned about you, put together your financial puzzle, and come up with some intelligent options to help you optimize your outcomes.

CHAPTER 5

OUR SECOND MEETING: WORKING ON A SOLUTION

Our second meeting is typically scheduled a week to 10 days after the first one. My team uses this time to research your financial situation, and look at all the puzzle pieces from every possible angle. We develop every solution "from scratch" – that is the only way to be sure that our recommendation are custom-tailored to you and your family.

You can expect that we will spend a portion of the second appointment going over the recommended solution. Together, we will make a decision on whether it makes sense for us to work together. If so, our next step will be implementing the financial strategy we have designed.

Do we sometimes turn prospects away?

The short answer is yes, we do. Here are two examples where, after the initial meeting and the research, we might decide that working together is not the best decision.

- **If your current advisor is doing a great job.**

My philosophy is, if it isn't broken, don't try to fix it! Sometimes, we perform "second opinion" reviews of financial strategies and investment portfolios and find them to be of sound design, well executed, and on track to get you to your goals. In that case, you have no need to switch advisors, and we will tell you as much.

- **If you are a "do it yourself" investor.**

Do it yourself clients do not typically mix well with our practice.

If you need to have your house re-wired, you call a licensed electrician and then stay out of his way. If you need surgery, you don't ask to be awake so that you can actively guide the surgeon as he makes the cuts and places the stitches. Investing is no different.

Our strength is hearing the client's concerns and preferences, developing a strategy, and then implementing it – while keeping the client informed and engaged. That requires a degree of trust from the client. If you believe deep inside that you will do a better job of managing your own money, working with us would be frustrating for both of us.

Barring those two scenarios, odds are that our

team can come up with a plan of action that has the potential to improve your financial and emotional outcomes. We treat every prospect as a client and a part of our practice – and do our review with care, thoughtfulness, and an eye towards creating the best possible results.

Importance of asking questions

Here is the most important thing I need you to know about the second meeting. As we walk you through our recommendations, please ask any and all questions that are on your mind. We want you to be confident in your understanding of what we are trying to accomplish together.

Here is an example from the recent past that points to people not asking nearly enough simple and obvious questions: Bernie Madoff. Madoff managed investor money by reportedly investing it in the market and generating consistently high returns. His investment method was marketed as too complex for outsiders to understand.

What was actually going on? Today we know that Bernie Madoff perpetrated what amounted to an elaborate Ponzi scheme. Early investors were paid using the money from later investors, until the entire $64.8 billion pyramid collapsed.[7]

I sometimes wonder what would have happened if investors had asked more, simple questions, and had not stopped until they could actually understand the answers. In reality, very smart and

---

[7] https://en.wikipedia.org/wiki/Madoff_investment_scandal

knowledgeable people could not understand how Bernie was doing it. That was a big red flag.

So, please, ask your questions. Even if you think they are dumb. Even if you think you really should know or be able to figure out the answer. This is your money, and I believe that every client has the capacity to grasp how that money can work for him. I promise we will never judge you for asking for clarification.

In addition to going over the recommended strategy, we will suggest the optimal way of working together. Different clients want and need a different degree of interaction with our office. Some want to talk monthly, others are perfectly happy with a conversation once a year. Depending on your personality and your needs, we will recommend an

THE PROCESS: YOUR PATH TO FINANCIAL WELLNESS

approach that we think will serve you best. Your opinion counts, of course.

If you are comfortable with the strategy and happy to move forward with our help, we will prepare the paperwork to get your assets moved. This process is really simple, and we will notify various financial institutions to transfer the funds for you. If you are coming to us from another advisor, we will handle all notifications and communications – there is nothing you need to do.

Jim and the Alamo Honor Flight guardians escorting WWII veterans through SA Airport for the flight to Washington DC.

Jim visiting with a Navy Veteran at the WWII memorial

WWII Memorial

THE PROCESS: YOUR PATH TO FINANCIAL WELLNESS

Arlington National Cemetery, changing of the guard.

Jim addressing the veterans at the WWII memorial and introducing General Parker.

THE PROCESS: YOUR PATH TO FINANCIAL WELLNESS

Vietnam veterans memorial

JIM HANNA

Iwo Jima

The Price of Freedom

JIM HANNA

CHAPTER 6

OUR THIRD MEETING:

FINALIZING THE DETAILS

The third meeting takes place about a week after the second one. In the time between the appointments, our team coordinates the money transfers and the account set-up.

During the appointment, we will go over the final allocations, double-check all the details, and ensure that everyone is on the same page.

From that point on, you and your family will always know when to expect an update from our team. Our job is to keep you on track – so, we put our expertise, experience, and understanding of your financial circumstances to work for your benefit.

Of course, your calls and questions are welcome any time – please don't feel like you have to wait until the next scheduled opportunity to get clarification. If something unexpected happens, such as a market bump, we will contact you right away to keep you informed.

You should know that we don't limit our interactions with you as a client to formal portfolio review calls a few times a year. Our office is well-known for hosting a variety of events for clients – from wine and cheese receptions to family barbeques and cooking classes. We enjoy getting to know you and your family in a laid-back setting. In our experience, this is particularly helpful for building relationships with spouses. We want for your entire family to feel that we will be there to support all of you.

Client relationships evolve and often include more and more family members, services, and responsibilities. The story of Bob and Sally is a perfect way to illustrate that.

Bob came into our office about 3 years ago. Bob (65 at the time) and his brother Tom were looking for a way to take care of their 91-year-old mother. By studying mom's financial situation in depth, we were able to get her a VA benefit. We reviewed her investments portfolio and made some changes to help protect her from market swings. We also worked with an attorney to prepare an estate plan and documents for her, making sure that her wishes were written down and assets were appropriately titled.

A few months after the work was done, we got an update call from Bob – his mom's health took a turn for the worse, and Bob was moving her to an assisted living facility. She passed away the next day. I went to the funeral. In sorting out his mom's affairs, all of her accounts and assets bypassed probate and went to the right beneficiaries – our estate planning work had paid off.

Thirty days after the funeral, Bob came into the office with his wife Sally. Bob shared that he had just been diagnosed with pancreatic cancer. He had not been sick a day in his life, so the news came as a complete shock. What he wanted the most was to make sure that Sally would be taken care of after he passed away. We did the planning work and got all accounts in order. Three months later, I was at Bob's funeral.

Had we not done the planning work beforehand, Sally would have been left in the lurch. Between taxes and probate, she would have had to deal with unexpected expenses and a whole lot of challenges in an emotionally trying time. Because of Bob's foresight, Sally now has an income stream that will last her a lifetime.

I tell this story because it highlights the importance of reviewing your financial situation with a trusted advisor. You never know what will happen next — your robust health today is not a guarantee of what tomorrow will look like. That is why we take a holistic approach, bring in a team of tax and estate specialists, look at your long term care plan, and ask difficult questions. This is our due diligence, and the way we take care of our client families. After all, we are here for the long term.

CHAPTER 7

CHOOSING THE RIGHT FINANCIAL ADVISOR FOR YOU

The choice of a financial advisor is an important one. After all, you will be trusting this professional to hold you accountable, keep you on track, and make astute decisions in your best interest. A simple check of qualifications won't do, although it is a part of the process. Here are the steps that I recommend taking when you are looking for a financial advisor.

Ask around for recommendations.

Your family, friends, and co-workers collectively know a lot of people. If someone is working with an advisor they love, you will find out by simply asking.

Make sure that their glowing recommendation is a result of a long-term relationship, not just one recent lucky win.

Do your homework.

The Internet makes it easy to research the background of any financial advisor.

The advisor's website is a great next thing to read – it will give you more details about the office, the investing philosophy, and the advisor. Keep in mind that the website is written by someone in the advisor's practice, so it presents a "best light" picture. Nonetheless, it should give you a sense for what to expect.

You may also do an Internet search for "(broker name) scam" (or fraud, conviction, allegation, etc.)

More likely than not, your search won't turn up anything at all, which is a good indicator. In the rare event that it does, whatever you find is worth investigating further. Integrity is not optional.

Choose a fiduciary advisor.

Remember that a broker is only required to recommend investments that are suitable for you. A broker is under no obligation to disclose conflicts of interest, and does not have to continue monitoring the recommended investment and your financial situation to be sure that the recommendation still makes sense three years from now.

An investment adviser representative is a fiduciary and is legally required to disclose any conflicts of interest that may exist, and to work under complete transparency. He or she must look at the entirety of your financial situation, and monitor it continually to be sure that your strategy and portfolio accurately reflect your changing circumstances. **Retire with Jim Hanna Wealth Advisors** is a fiduciary practice.

Pay attention during the meetings.

The initial meetings offer a great opportunity for you to assess whether the advisor is a good fit. Does he or she listen well? Is there a focus on your holistic financial health picture – beyond just savings accounts and Social Security? In my experience, an office that can bring in a CPA or an attorney to help you with a complex tax question or an estate planning document can become a wonderful one-stop resource for your family.

On that note, be sure that the advisor involves both you and your spouse in the conversation. That goes beyond the obligatory nod in the beginning of the meeting and a handshake at the end! You are in this together, and chances are that one of you will be left to manage the financial situation when the other one passes. Be sure you are both comfortable in the interactions with the advisor.

Remember that you can understand your investments.

Your advisor will always have more technical knowledge about investments – after all, that is his job. However, I believe that every single client has the capacity to understand what his or her investments are, why the money is allocated the way it is, and how the strategy is designed to help him work towards his financial goals. If you do not have that understanding, keep asking questions. If your advisor cannot explain your choices in simple terms you can understand, and do it patiently, you may be better off looking elsewhere.

Know how your advisor gets paid.

Financial advisors are professionals that make a living helping families manage their money. Some advisors charge a fee for the initial consultation while others are paid a percentage of the assets they manage. Some advisors make money by selling specific financial products. In order to make an informed decision, you must have a clear understanding of how the advisor gets paid, and how much the fee is. No one likes surprises!

Here is a client story that will illustrate the importance of understanding exactly how your financial advisor gets paid.

Victoria and Ray first joined us at one of our informational presentations and then attended a two day retirement workshop I hosted at a local college. They were getting closer to retirement and were reaching out on their own for as much information as they could to help them prepare.

Victoria and Ray are a well-educated, unassuming couple in their early 60's. They live modestly despite the fact that they are worth several million dollars. Their primary concern was to protect what they had.

They were also looking for ways to reduce their tax expenses.

As we recommend to all of our new clients, Victoria and Ray brought in their account statements for our review. The couple had an advisor with a large firm managing their portfolio for over 10 years, and Ray was concerned that they hadn't seen much growth on their assets through that time. After running a third party report, we found out something quite shocking.

Our analysis uncovered a significant number of fees that the couple had been paying. Some of those fees were never spelled out in a prospectus or supplement to a prospectus! Victoria and Ray had no idea that they were being charged in excess of $50,000 per year in fees - that's over $500,000 in fees over a ten year period! It's no wonder they had not seen much growth in their portfolio – the fees were consuming whatever gains they may have had!

Needless to say they were furious with their advisor at the time, who they promptly fired.

We put together a full financial strategy for them, and implemented strategies that not only lowered their fees by thousands of dollars but also repositioned some assets into tax deferred buckets to save on taxes.

If the couple had not had the confidence in our firm to ask for a second opinion, they would have continued paying those exorbitant fees. It is possible that they would not have figured this out for several more years, resulting in additional losses.

Retirement dollars are precious. No one will give you a raise once you start drawing them down, so you want to accumulate sufficient retirement funds to last a lifetime. Fees, along with inflation, are two deal killers that you must investigate and plan for.

There are many people who have managed to accumulate large portfolios. However, it doesn't mean they know everything that is happening in those portfolios behind the scenes. You must ask the right questions and request an independent review when in doubt. The financial services industry is complicated with all of its acronyms and regulatory changes. Products and industry tools become outdated and are replaced all the time. It is a full time job for those of us in the business to stay abreast of the very best tools and strategies out there for our clients. As a client without a financial background, you cannot possibly be expected to sort this out on your own. So, seek advice – but be sure you understand what it will cost you.

Be clear about what to expect when it comes to client service.

Many advisor offices juggle serving over two hundred households. Ask the advisor what his or her typical client interaction schedule looks like. Some prefer to schedule brief quarterly review phone calls, others like to do a single annual face to face meeting. Some offices offer multiple interaction opportunities during the year from cheese and wine tastings to family barbeques (our office happens to be one of those).

There is no single right way to deliver good client service. You must choose the advisor who offers an interaction frequency that is right for you.

And now, since we have covered our thoughts on the right way to choose a great financial advisor, let's talk about some red flags. How do you know when you might be talking to an advisor that is not a good choice for you?

CHAPTER 8

RED FLAGS IN A FINANCIAL ADVISOR

While my general guidance on this is to go with your gut, there are some obvious red flags that can serve as an early warning. Here is a list.

The advisor is a poor listener.

In order to recommend investments that are a good fit for your financial situation, an advisor must understand who you are. He or she must know what your goals look like, what resources you have, and how much risk you are comfortable with.

That is a lot to absorb, so a good advisor spends the first meeting or two listening intently. The truth is that a good advisor never really stops listening. If you get a sense that you are not being heard, if you have to repeat yourself, or if the recommendations clearly go against your preferences, you need to interview someone else.

The advisor cranks up the sales pressure.

This red flag can look like a sales push of a particular product. It may also show up as a "Limited time opportunity, you must sign up today or you will regret it for the rest of your life!" pitch. Sometimes an advisor might try to bully you into something that you are not ready for.

Either way, sales pressure is not OK. This is not a used car dealership – your financial independence and lifestyle are on the line! Hard selling is an early sign that the advisor does not have your best interest in mind, and is probably after a commission. You don't have to tolerate that.

The advisor offers to manage your investments "for free".

Remember what they say about the free cheese and the mousetrap! No professional service is ever truly free. Managing your financial life is a full-time job, and a legitimate advisor gets paid for doing it.

What a "free" offer usually means is that the advisor gets a commission or a kick-back payment from the manufacturers of the products that he or she sells you, but is not charging you a recurring asset management fee. It could also mean that he or she is not willing to be honest with you about the compensation arrangements. My advice? Say "No thank you!" and walk away.

The advisor is unable to explain financial vehicles in simple terms.

This can show up as exasperation at your questions, an inability to finish a sentence without using jargon, or "Just sign here, I will explain later". An advisor who understands your situation, investment strategy, and the financial products he or she solicits will find a way of explaining things in plain English. If you are talking to someone who is trying to drown you in technical words, numbers, and charts, walk away. You deserve to understand what your money is doing for you.

The advisor is dismissive of your spouse.

This does not happen much these days, but I have seen it and heard my clients complain about this treatment in other offices. Your spouse is an integral part of the financial decisions for the family. If an advisor limits his conversation and questions to you, and is dismissive or condescending towards your spouse ("What does she know?") that is not acceptable. You are looking for an advisor who will respect and support you both.

The advisor is disorganized or disrespectful of your time.

Life happens. Sometimes even the most organized offices run behind schedule. However, if you are observing a consistent trend of running late, missing appointments, rescheduling at the last minute, and not being able to locate your files or notes, you may be dealing with an office that does not have its ducks in a row. Would you trust your tax preparation to a CPA who routinely misplaces the receipts you brought in, misses deadlines, and makes mistakes in adding up the numbers? Of course not. The same holds true for a financial advisor.

A lack of transparency.

I like to refer to it as "the shady factor". If the advisor is evasive in answering direct questions (think more political debate than informative response), I would begin to wonder what he or she is trying to hide. It is possible that the advisor is just not a good communicator, but even that mostly benign trait can spell trouble when you are dealing with finances. You must have clear, transparent answers on important decision points – like independence, conflicts of interest, and how the advisor gets compensated.

Big promises and guarantees that seem too good to be true.

If it seems too good to be true, it probably isn't true! Many advisors are proud of their track record of successful money management, and they are legally allowed to talk about historical performance, trends, and scenarios. However, if someone outright promises or guarantees to outperform the market, he or she is overstepping what is legally allowed. Confidence is a good thing, but a cocky or brash attitude is not something you want to see when it comes to your money.

In summary, pay attention in the early meetings – these are your reconnaissance trips, an opportunity to test-drive what it will be like to work with this advisor. Think of it as dating. If you don't like the way the first few dates go and you feel disrespected, lied to or just uneasy, you won't propose marriage. Choosing a financial advisor is no different. Even though the conversation may touch on difficult subjects, the general tone should be one of respect, understanding, and support. If you are not getting that from your advisor, find one that will do it right.

CHAPTER 9

JIM HANNA'S TEAM – AMBASSADOR EXPERIENCE

Retire with Jim Hanna Wealth Advisors is an independent financial services firm. We serve people who are approaching or are in retirement. Our mission since 1981 has been to help them create financial clarity and to improve the quality of their lives. Our practice has been in San Antonio since inception, and we remain rooted in community and focused on relationships.

Since 2007, I have been involved in assisting veterans obtain VA benefits. I have been granted authority by the Department of Veteran Affairs to assist with veteran claims, and I pride myself on helping fellow veterans find their way through the VA system.

Whatever a prospective client's situation, we begin with a holistic assessment of his or her circumstances. Here are some of the services we offer.

- Retirement income strategies
- Wealth accumulation
- Annuities
- Life insurance
- Asset protection
- Tax-reduction strategies

Most clients come to us with a specific "pain" or concern they want addressed. Some are uncertain they can afford to retire. Others want to explore their options when it comes to creating their own steady and reliable stream of income payments to cover their living expenses. We involve our whole team of specialists in a conversation that considers solutions from every possible angle, so that our recommendations are well-informed.

Our Client's Bill of Rights

Our clients get more than one-time advice. As fiduciaries, we continually look at their personal and financial circumstances so that our advice is always in their best interests.

To set expectations and help you understand what your experience will be like as a prospect and a client, we have compiled this short *Client's Bill of*

Rights. In a straightforward way, it conveys the experience of our clients. Some of these points may seem obvious, and yet there is value in spelling them out as our commitment to you.

1. I expect my advisor to tell the truth and be on my side.
2. I expect my advisor to understand my financial and personal situation, including my circumstances, goals and values.
3. I expect my advisor to help me make good choices and avoid making mistakes.
4. I expect my advisor to keep me informed. I deserve to have my phone calls and messages returned promptly.

5. I expect my advisor to explain complex financial concepts in plain English that I can understand.

6. We are all human. Should a mistake happen, I expect that my advisor will acknowledge and correct it without delay.

7. My family and I deserve to be treated with respect and integrity at all times.

8. I deserve honest advice and feedback, even when it may be hard to hear.

9. I trust that my advisor is knowledgeable and up to date on important developments and changes that may affect me.

10. I have the right to the strictest level of confidentiality in regards to my financial and personal information.

As you have seen throughout this book, we are here to serve your family. We will involve your spouse to be sure that you both understand how your money is working for you.

Our approach to client contact is staying in touch continuously. We conduct regular portfolio reviews and updates to give you an opportunity to ask questions, revisit strategy, and correct our course if your situation changes. We also organize many informal events for client families, from summer barbeques to wine tasting socials. We want you to know that we are here for you.

THE PROCESS: YOUR PATH TO FINANCIAL WELLNESS

A few words about Jim Hanna

I have a bit of an unusual biography for a financial advisor. Before helping people sort out their finances, I served in the Air Force as a C130 Crew Chief from 1963 to 1967, my crew and I spent most of that time in and out of Vietnam.

I am the CEO and founder of **Retire with Jim Hanna Wealth Advisors**. I have 34 years of experience in the insurance and financial industry. I hold my general lines agent insurance license and am an Investment Adviser Representative in the state of Texas.

As an experienced Veterans Accredited Claims Agent, my passion for assisting veterans and their spouses has allowed me to assist with hundreds of claims. This has resulted with over $20 million in annualized benefits to veterans or surviving spouses – a result I am very proud of.

I live in Pipe Creek, Texas, with my wife, Barbie, and our two dogs, Carly the black lab, and Jasper the yellow lab. Outside of the office, I enjoy deep-sea fishing and participating in wildlife preservation. I am also a board member of a non-profit animal rescue mission focusing on military service dogs. My team and I are proud sponsors of Guide Dogs of Texas, the only guide dog school in Texas that provides guide dogs to the visually impaired.

Made in the USA
Monee, IL
06 September 2023